cenyp

PROGRESSIVISM,
the GREAT DEPRESSION,
and the NEW DEAL

1901–1941

PROGRESSIVISM,
the GREAT DEPRESSION,
and the NEW DEAL

1901–1941

Christopher Collier
James Lincoln Collier

BENCHMARK BOOKS

MARSHALL CAVENDISH
NEW YORK

ACKNOWLEDGMENT: The authors wish to thank Alan Brinkley, Professor of History, Columbia University, for his careful reading of the text of this volume of The Drama of American History and his thoughtful and useful comments. The work has been much improved by Professor Brinkley's notes. The authors are deeply in his debt, but, of course, assume full responsibility for the substance of the work, including any errors that may appear.

Photo research by James Lincoln Collier.
COVER PHOTO: *Corbis/Bettmann*
PICTURE CREDITS: The photographs in this book are used by permission and through the courtesy of: *Corbis/Bettmann:* 10, 11, 16, 23, 38, 40, 46, 47, 51, 56, 57, 59 (top & bottom), 60, 64, 65, 71, 72, 73, 77, 81, 83, 84; *Library of Congress:* 50; *New York Public Library:* 12, 13 (left & right), 15, 20, 25, 27, 28, 30, 33 (left & right), 37 (left & right), 53, 66.

Benchmark Books
Marshall Cavendish Corporation
99 White Plains Road
Tarrytown, New York 10591-9001

Library of Congress Cataloging-in-Publication Data

Collier, Christopher, 1930-
Progressivism, the Great Depression, and the New Deal, 1901 to 1941
/ by Christopher Collier, James Lincoln Collier.
p. cm. — (The drama of American history)
Includes bibliographical references and index.
ISBN 0-7614-1054-6
1. United States—History—1901-1953—Juvenile literature. 2. United States—Politics and government—1901-1953—Juvenile literature. 3. Progressivism (United States politics)—History—20th century—Juvenile literature. 4. Depressions—1929—United States—Juvenile literature. 5. New Deal, 1933-1939—Juvenile literature. [1. Progressivism (United States politics) 2. Depressions—1929. 3. New Deal, 1933-1939. 4. United States—History—1901-1953. 5. United States—Politics and government—1901-1953.]
I. Collier, James Lincoln, 1928-   . II. Title.
E741 .C53 2000
973.91—dc21
00-029481
Printed in the United States of America
1 3 5 6 4 2

CONTENTS

PREFACE

Over many years of both teaching and writing for students at all levels, from grammar school to graduate school, it has been borne in on us that many, if not most, American history textbooks suffer from trying to include everything of any moment in the history of the nation. Students become lost in a swamp of factual information, and as a consequence lose track of how those facts fit together and why they are significant and relevant to the world today.

In this series, our effort has been to strip the vast amount of available detail down to a central core. Our aim is to draw in bold strokes, providing enough information, but no more than is necessary, to bring out the basic themes of the American story, and what they mean to us now. We believe that it is surely more important for students to grasp the underlying concepts and ideas that emerge from the movement of history, than to memorize an array of facts and figures.

The difference between this series and many standard texts lies in what has been left out. We are convinced that students will better remember the important themes if they are not buried under a heap of names, dates, and places.

In this sense, our primary goal is what might be called citizenship education. We think it is critically important for America as a nation and Americans as individuals to understand the origins and workings of the public institutions that are central to American society. We have asked ourselves again and again what is most important for citizens of our democracy to know so they can most effectively make the system work for them and the nation. For this reason, we have focused on political and institutional history, leaving social and cultural history less well developed.

This series is divided into volumes that move chronologically through the American story. Each is built around a single topic, such as the Pilgrims, the Constitutional Convention, or immigration. Each volume has been written so that it can stand alone, for students who wish to research a given topic. As a consequence, in many cases material from previous volumes is repeated, usually in abbreviated form, to set the topic in its historical context. That is to say, students of the Constitutional Convention must be given some idea of relations with England, and why the Revolution was fought, even though the material was covered in detail in a previous volume. Readers should find that each volume tells an entire story that can be read with or without reference to other volumes.

Despite our belief that it is of the first importance to outline sharply basic concepts and generalizations, we have not neglected the great dramas of American history. The stories that will hold the attention of students are here, and we believe they will help the concepts they illustrate to stick in their minds. We think, for example, that knowing of Abraham Baldwin's brave and dramatic decision to vote with the small states at the Constitutional Convention will bring alive the Connecticut Compromise, out of which grew the American Senate.

Each of these volumes has been read by esteemed specialists in its particular topic; we have benefited from their comments.

CHAPTER I

The Struggle to Come

The Great Depression of the 1930s was one of the worst calamities to hit the United States in its entire history. Probably only the Civil War brought more misery to so many Americans. Almost everybody was affected by the Depression, and a great many people lost everything, many never to fully recover. Today unemployment much above 6 percent is considered unacceptable, and over 10 percent won't be tolerated. During the Depression a *quarter*, and by some estimates, a third, of all American workers were out of jobs. Many of those who had jobs were working reduced hours, and almost every worker had taken a significant pay cut. Thousands of boys and girls as young as ten and twelve were homeless, wandering about the country, the girls often dressed as boys for safety. Others were living in shacks in shantytowns on the outskirts of cities.

There had been depressions, or financial "panics," before, but none so severe or long lasting. In earlier depressions, the main sufferers had been laboring people; the middle class had usually been able to scrape by. But in the Great Depression of the 1930s the middle class, too, suffered. Many professionals, like lawyers, business executives, and accountants,

There had been financial "panics" in the United States from time to time. This cartoon, from the nineteenth century, shows the "Puck Boy" of Puck magazine burying his money while the background banks totter.

found themselves begging for pick-and-shovel jobs, or selling apples on street corners. Millions of families lost their homes and had to take small apartments or move in with parents or other relatives. Few people actually starved to death, but many families ate cheap foods like spaghetti and rice night after night, and had for breakfast coffee and perhaps a roll. People got used to wearing shoes with holes in their soles, stuffing a piece of cardboard inside the shoe to cover the hole. By the standards of the Depression, people considered poor today would have been thought well-off.

The Depression dramatically changed the way Americans saw their government. As a consequence, the government itself changed. America now is a different nation from what it had been before the Depression. The effect of the Depression on the United States is the story of this book. It is a long and complicated story: Even today, decades later, historians and economists argue about the causes of the Depression and what it has meant to Americans. In order to understand the causes, we must step a long way back, to the latter decades of the 1800s, and over the next four

The Depression of the 1930s touched almost everybody. Suddenly impoverished businessmen found themselves selling apples on street corners to get a little money to buy food for their families.

chapters look at the sequence of events that led to the terrifying stock market crash of 1929 and the Depression that followed.

★ ★ ★

We can begin in about 1870, when the United States was an agricultural nation, with the bulk of Americans living on farms, most of them single-family farms with perhaps a hired hand or two. Although by 1870 a great many things that had previously been made at home were store-bought, many farm families were still fairly self-sufficient, and, instead of buying many consumer items, could get along on what they made at home.

But already by 1870 American was becoming *urbanized* and *industrialized*. That is to say, more and more people were leaving the farms and flocking to the cities, where they worked in factories, in mines, or on railroads and ships, instead of in fields or barns. (For more detail on this change, readers can consult the volumes in this series called *The Rise of Industry* and *The Rise of the Cities*.) Now, instead of working for themselves, they had jobs in companies and corporations. Now, instead of

For centuries America had been an agricultural nation, with the vast majority of Americans growing their own food and making most of what they needed. But as this 1872 painting shows, even by then factories were beginning to take over.

growing or making what they needed, they had to buy most things. As scholars put it, more and more Americans were becoming enmeshed in the *market economy*. They worked for wages, making things that were sold throughout the nation, and bought what they needed. They were part of a very complex system over which they had little control—which indeed seemed, even to people fairly high up in it, to have a mind of its own. Inevitably in complex systems a change to one small part may affect the whole system.

Industrial systems can be run with greater or lesser amounts of government regulation. The amount of government regulation over business in most nations fluctuates over time; but in most industrial nations there is at least some government control over business, and in some industri-

As these two advertisements show, by the end of the nineteenth century Americans were buying a great many products they had once made at home.

al nations a fair amount of it. In the 1800s in America, when industry was growing, there was very little government control. By the end of the century, a very small percentage of people ended up owning the corporations, with their factories, mines, railroads, oil wells, and such, where about half of the laborers worked.

It was obvious that the owners of factories could increase profits by keeping wages for workers low and demanding that they work long hours. They were able to do this because during the second half of the 1800s there were always plenty of new workers coming into the cities asking for jobs. Many of these were from farms, trying to escape harsh conditions there. (We shall learn more about farm problems shortly.) Millions of others were flooding in from outside as immigrants, mainly from Europe, but also from China, Japan, and Canada. With so many workers competing for jobs, corporate managers could keep wages down and hours long by playing off the workers against each other. In 1900 average earnings for workers were between $300 and $400 a year. Shop girls in Boston earned $5 to $6 a week. Women sewing at home might earn 30 cents to 40 cents a day. Money was worth more in those days; still, $5 a week was not enough to support even one person in 1900. Inevitably, somewhere between 10 and 20 million Americans were poor, even by these very low standards—that is, they were not eating enough of the right kind of food to maintain their weight. (The population of the United States in 1900 was 76 million.)

Farmers were not much better off than industrial laborers, and in many cases were worse off. By the 1880s the old self-sufficient farm had pretty much disappeared. Instead of keeping a few fruit trees for apples and pears, a kitchen garden for turnips and squash, a cow for milk, and chickens for eggs, farmers were growing single crops like wheat, sugar, and cotton, which they would sell to businesses and then buy what they needed with the money. Farmers, thus, were also being enmeshed in the market economy. They needed railroads to carry their goods to market,

Through the nineteenth century the United States became increasingly a nation of cities and factories. By the 1870s industrialization was changing the American way of life.

manufacturers to mill their wheat into flour, spin their cotton into yarn, turn their hogs into canned ham and bacon. Pioneers pushing west were opening up more and more land to farming, and new inventions, like harvesting machines and hay balers, were making farms more efficient. As a consequence, America was producing an oversupply of food. This food glut had to be sold overseas. Unhappily for American farmers, Russia, Canada, Australia, and other nations were also producing food surpluses. The price of agricultural produce dropped, and dropped again. Just to take one example, in 1866 wheat brought the farmer $1.45 a bushel; by 1889 it was down to 69 cents a bushel, and by 1894, down to 49 cents a bushel. The prices of corn, cotton, hogs, and virtually every other farm product fell in the same way.

With industrialization came poverty and slums. These two boys, without shoes and wearing tattered clothes, were typical of millions who were living in the worst sort of conditions in American cities.

Overproduction was not the only problem. Another was that railroads were charging farmers exorbitant prices for carrying their goods to big-city markets. In the West especially there was often only a single railroad line servicing a given area. Farmers in that area either shipped on the local line or not at all. The line could charge almost any price it wanted and, not surprisingly, shipping prices were high. Sometimes it was cheaper for farmers to burn their corn for fuel than ship it to market.

Nature, too, was being unhelpful: The second half of the 1800s saw a succession of droughts, terrible winters, plagues of locusts. Still using old-fashioned methods, farmers let their land erode until it was filled with gullies, the rich topsoil washed away. No wonder so many young people left the farms for jobs in the cities. (For the story of the farmers' problems in this era, see the volume in this series called *Indians, Cowboys, and Farmers and the Battle for the Great Plains.*)

By the 1890s, if not before, it was clear to both farmers and workers that they were living very hard lives indeed, while a small handful of people were growing rich from their labor. Yet there was another viewpoint. It was clearly true that the American industrial machine was creating great wealth for the nation. Even though this wealth was not being fairly shared, most people were better off in 1900 than their parents had been thirty years earlier. Further, it seemed likely that the industrial machine would continue to produce more and more, as in fact it did. Thus, it appeared to many thoughtful people that while the *capitalist system* of free enterprise had its flaws, on the whole it worked to everybody's good in the long run. Therefore, it would be best to let it go on unhindered by government. Of course there were inequalities; but according to this viewpoint, a certain measure of inequality was inevitable in any system.

The term for this idea of unfettered business is *laissez-faire*, a French term meaning, roughly, to "let alone." (It is pronounced *lay-say fair*.) Boiled down, laissez-faire meant that the government ought to let businesses alone to operate as their owners and managers wished. Competition among companies would force them to keep prices down and improve their products in order to attract buyers.

Businessmen understood well enough that while competition might benefit the country as a whole, it did not benefit them individually. So they worked out schemes to cut down on competition. They might quietly agree to keep their prices all the same, at a high level. They might combine several smaller companies into one gigantic one, thus getting a *monopoly*. In its pure sense, a monopoly controls the total production or supply of a commodity. For practical purposes, however, a monopoly is said to exist if one company can control the price of a commodity or service. U.S. Steel, formed by J.P. Morgan, and Standard Oil, formed by John D. Rockefeller, were nearly complete monopolies. There were other, more complicated schemes for avoiding competition. While the competitive system might work in theory, in practice businessmen often found ways around it.

Thus, farmers and laborers were being squeezed twice by the corporation: Employers were paying the lowest possible wages to workers, and processors were paying the lowest prices to farmers for their produce; and they were charging the highest possible prices for the things farmers and working families had to buy.

But there was yet one more squeeze. In those days there were no income taxes. The federal government got most of its money from *tariffs*—taxes on goods imported into the United States. Tariffs had a secondary use. If set high enough, they would push the price of foreign-made goods up so high that they couldn't be profitably sold in the United States. High tariffs were used to protect American manufacturers in many industries. Without foreign competition to drive prices down, prices of many goods were kept artificially high, as was the case with such necessities as sugar, steel, textiles.

By the late 1800s farmers and laborers had become conscious of what seemed to them the unfairness of the system and began to fight back. Farmers formed alliances, workers joined unions. Workers struck again and again, demanding higher wages and shorter hours. Between 1881 and 1906 there were some 38,000 strikes and lockouts, involving 9.5 million workers. (A lockout is when, threatened by a strike, the business owners shut down their factories temporarily.) Some of these strikes were vicious and bitter. In 1892, during a strike against the Carnegie Steel Company in Homestead, Pennsylvania, the company brought in a private army and blood was spilled. A railroad strike in 1894 paralyzed the nation's transport system for several weeks, until the government brought in troops to quell the strike with much violence.

In the end, neither the workers through their unions, nor the farmers through their organizations, could prevail: Wages remained low, prices high, hours long. Why, when the farmers and laborers were the majority of Americans, could they not change things?

To begin with, most Americans, especially businessmen, believed firmly in laissez-faire—that in the long run the capitalist system would work to the benefit of everybody if government let business alone. But other businessmen simply did not care about the public good; they were solely interested in getting as rich as possible. The railroad baron Commodore Vanderbilt said, "Law? What do I care about law? Haven't I got the power?" Andrew Carnegie, the steel magnate, said, "The workers have no more to say about their wages than does a piece of coal about its price."

Unfortunately for the farmers and workers, government officials generally took the side of business against labor. There were several reasons for this. For one, businessmen supported with campaign contributions candidates who agreed with them. Sometimes they even bribed judges, state legislators, even U.S. congressmen to vote their way. Furthermore, government officials tended to come from the same social class as businessmen—in fact, they often had businesses in their families or were businessmen themselves. They naturally took a pro-business point of view.

Again, many people, even including many farmers and workers, believed that strikes and such were caused by foreign "agitators." There was a certain truth to this. Many of the union leaders and strike organizers were immigrants, or from immigrant families. A lot of them had brought from Europe socialist ideas that government ought to have some control over wages, hours, and prices. Finally, the strikes, and riots that sometimes came along with the strikes, troubled many Americans; it sometimes almost seemed as if the nation were on the edge of revolution or chaos. Many workers themselves agreed with this. In fact, a lot of workers hoped to start small businesses themselves—a tailor shop, a fish pushcart—and rise up in the capitalist system. Such people supported the idea of laissez-faire.

It is not surprising then that most government officials felt they had a duty to stop strikes when they could. An example of how government worked against organized labor came in the infamous Pullman strike.

A sketch of the first meat train leaving the Chicago stockyards during the railroad strike of 1894. The government has provided a cavalry escort to prevent strikers from stopping the train.

The Pullman Company made sleeping and parlor cars that it rented to railroads. In 1894 the Pullman workers went on strike. The American Railroad Union decided to support the Pullman workers. They would not handle any train that included Pullman cars, and in the end paralyzed the railroad system in the North. There was a lot of disorder and President Grover Cleveland decided to step in. His excuse was that the strikers were preventing a lot of mail from getting through. He said, "If it takes every dollar in the Treasury and every soldier in the United States to deliver a postal card in Chicago, that postal card should be delivered." As it happened, Cleveland's attorney general, Richard Olney, had been a lawyer for a railroad. His office persuaded a judge to issue a court order against the leaders of the American Railway Union—in particular, its president, Eugene Debs—saying they mustn't hold up the mails. In response, strikers interrupted a mail train and took over some railroad switching plants in Chicago. The government then called in soldiers. When Debs refused to call off the strike, he was sent to jail for six months, and within weeks the strike collapsed.

What happened in the railroad strike happened in many others. The government sent in soldiers, or got court orders jailing strike leaders. In some cases the strikers won, but in most cases they did not; and when they did win their gains were usually slight, involving a small increase in pay, or a somewhat shorter day.

By 1890 it was clear to workers and farmers alike that they had to get the government on their side. Thus began a battle for the mind of the government—and the American people—on a central issue that is still being fought over today. That issue was whether the government has a responsibility to see that all citizens are treated fairly, by setting limits on what corporations can do, or whether it should stay out of the way and let issues work themselves out without government interference. How much government interference in the economy was appropriate was a question that would become crucial during the Great Depression of the 1930s.

CHAPTER II

The Progressive Era

By 1900, if not before, it had become obvious to many thoughtful people that too many Americans were not getting their fair share of the growing American prosperity. Among them was a group of journalists who came to be called "muckrakers": Ida Tarbell, Lincoln Steffens, Jacob Riis, and others, who set out to expose the harsh tactics of many industries. They also wrote about the terrible slum conditions in which millions of workers lived. The writings of the muckrakers had a substantial impact on the American public.

But for any change to take place, government had to take the lead. One man who was willing to do so was Theodore Roosevelt, a New York Republican born to a wealthy family. (He shouldn't be confused with his distant cousin, Franklin D. Roosevelt, who was president later.) Roosevelt went to Harvard, studied law briefly, and wrote on history. But he was an active, adventurous man, who went west to try the life of the cowboy, and fell in love with the open country. He went into government, fought in Cuba in the Spanish-American War, was elected governor of New York and in 1900 became vice president of the United States under William McKinley. In 1901 McKinley was assassinated by an anarchist, and Roosevelt became president.

Teddy Roosevelt, as everybody called him, had a sympathy for the underdog and wanted to curb the excesses of the corporations in order to aid ordinary people. His first move was to attack the monopolies, or "trusts," as they were called. Capitalism is based on the idea that competition will keep prices down and improve product quality, for the good of everybody. In a monopoly there is no effective competition, and the general good suffers. By 1900 in America businessmen in nearly all the major—and many minor—industries had managed to create monopolies.

In 1890, to curb monopolies, the government had passed the famous Sherman Antitrust Act, which allowed it to break them up. However, the Supreme Court, which supported the business point of view, had taken the teeth out of the antitrust laws through its decisions in a number of cases. Among other limiting decisions, it said that if the businesses involved were not engaged in interstate commerce, they were not under federal control; and if the monopoly grew out

Teddy Roosevelt was a hero to many Americans, who believed he would help them against the rich and powerful. This cartoon shows him forcing an important politician, Thomas Collier Platt, to do his bidding.

of the "natural workings of the market" rather than a conspiracy, it was perfectly legal.

Roosevelt attacked the monopolies where he could. Railroads were clearly engaged in interstate commerce, and Roosevelt succeeded in breaking up some railroad monopolies. A former ranch owner and cowboy, he won a decision against the "beef trust," which had been combining to set prices for cattle. In all, Roosevelt's government fought forty-four antitrust cases, winning some and losing some. (For a different side of Roosevelt's character see the volume in this series called *The United States Enters the World Stage*.)

Roosevelt also saw that government had often favored businesses over strikers, and he wanted to even the balance. In 1902 the United Mine Workers struck for a pay increase and shorter hours. The owners shut down the mines, hoping to starve the workers into submission. In those days, most houses and buildings were heated by coal. In October, Roosevelt called a conference at the White House of union leaders and mine owners. The mine owners came, but refused to speak to the union leaders. Roosevelt was enraged, threatened to take over the mines and have the army run them. This might have been illegal, but the mine owners were afraid Roosevelt would actually do it. Besides, a lot of Americans, workers themselves, supported the union. In the end the union got a raise and shorter hours. This was, however, an unusual outcome. In most cases the unions lost and Roosevelt did nothing to help them. Nevertheless, he was the first president to stand up to the great corporations.

Roosevelt's policies proved to be popular, and in 1904 he was elected by a large majority. Emboldened, he pushed his policies ever more forcefully. He devoted most of his 1905 annual message to Congress to the need for regulating business. Soon he got Congress to give the Interstate Commerce Commission, hitherto rather toothless, the power to set maximum freight rates for railroads, a blessing to farmers who were being overcharged.

Both state and the federal governments usually sided with business against workers. In 1912 during a textile strike in Lawrence, Massachusetts, the National Guard was called out to keep strikers in check. Roosevelt wanted to give the workers fair play.

Next he proposed controls over medicinal drugs. Many companies were selling "tonics" and "elixirs" that contained a lot of alcohol and other drugs, but would not cure anything. In 1906 Roosevelt pushed Congress into passing the Pure Food and Drug Act.

There were also problems in the meatpacking industry. Rats often ran wild over the meat as it lay in storage, and workers suffering from diseases like tuberculosis were allowed to handle meat. Americans had learned about such conditions from Upton Sinclair's popular novel, *The Jungle*. Even the most fervent believer in laissez-faire would admit that such unsanitary conditions could not be permitted, and in 1906 Congress passed a law allowing the government to inspect meat. Thus, in small increments, progressives—as these reformers called themselves—began to chip away at the laissez-faire system.

Because of his love for the western lands, Teddy Roosevelt was an ardent conservationist. Ranchers, miners, lumber companies, and others wanted a free hand to exploit the nation's natural resources, for their own profit, of course, but also to help the national economy expand. Roosevelt was determined that the beauties of the countryside should be preserved for all Americans. He was not the first to think of national parks: Yellowstone National Park had been created in 1872. But Roosevelt increased the public lands from 46 million acres to 172 million acres.

The policies followed by Teddy Roosevelt, taken together, have been termed "progressive," and the movement around them "progressivism." They were by no means original with Roosevelt, but had been developed by many people, like the muckrakers and progressive politicians over the years. But Roosevelt was responsible for pushing them through. Roosevelt was a very popular president, and his form of progressivism had the support of the majority of Americans. In the 1904 campaign Roosevelt had promised not to run again, and it is questionable that conservative Republican leaders would have nominated him anyway. To succeed himself, he handpicked his secretary of war, William Howard Taft. Taft, a big man weighing 340 pounds, pledged to carry on Roosevelt's progressive policies. Though he had never run for elective office before, Taft was easily elected.

Taft had been a judge, and was more a thinker than a doer like Roosevelt. Nonetheless, in many ways he followed progressive policies, fighting more antitrust cases than Roosevelt had, pushing through controls over telephone and telegraph rates, and getting a law passed requiring members of the House of Representatives to reveal who had con-

In 1908 Roosevelt decided to step down. He handpicked his successor, William Howard Taft, whom he felt would carry on his policies. Eventually he grew disillusioned with Taft, and again ran for the presidency, this time on the third-party "Bull Moose" ticket.

tributed money to their election campaigns.

But Taft was a conservative at heart, and on some issues, especially conservation, he backed away from progressive policies. Teddy Roosevelt felt betrayed, and in 1912 he decided to run as the candidate of the new Progressive Party. Roosevelt, as ever eager to do battle, said he was "roaring like a bull moose," and ever since, the party has been known as the Bull Moose Party. Roosevelt took a very strong stance against business in his speeches, saying that there had to be "thoroughgoing and effective regulation" of major industries, and "government supervision...of all corporations doing an interstate business."

Third parties do not usually do well in American elections. Despite his radical talk, Roosevelt's Bull Moose Party did better than most, coming in ahead of the regular Republican Party led by Taft. But with the

Republican vote split, the Democratic candidate slipped in with less than a majority of the popular vote.

He was Woodrow Wilson, considered by many people one of our greatest presidents. Wilson started his career as a lawyer, but quickly became a scholar and professor of history and political science. He went on to be president of Princeton University, and a governor of New Jersey. He was a quiet, studious man, wholly unlike the flamboyant Teddy Roosevelt, and politicians thought he would be easy to control. To the contrary, Wilson proved to be a man of high principle, iron determination, and unwillingness to compromise unless driven to the wall.

Wilson pressed successfully for a constitutional amendment requiring direct election of United States senators. In the past, state legislatures had chosen

With the Republican vote divided between Taft and Roosevelt, Woodrow Wilson slipped into the presidency. Like Roosevelt, he was determined to give ordinary Americans a fairer chance against the powerful industrialists who controlled the factories and other workplaces.

senators; now the people would vote for them directly. Next, Wilson went after what was called the "money trust"—powerful combinations of bankers that could control the nation's economy by manipulating the supply of money, and even the value of gold and silver. The bankers fought hard against government controls on them, but in the end Congress passed the Owen-Glass Act, setting up the Federal Reserve System, which exists today with much enlarged powers and responsibilities. The Federal Reserve System, in its original form, attempted, among other things, to control inflation by setting basic interest rates and adjusting the money supply, and regulated banks that held charters from the national, rather than the state, government.

Then in 1914 Wilson pushed through an act creating the Federal Trade Commission, still in existence. The FTC, as it is generally known, was given the power to investigate corporations and businessmen, and to order them to stop what it considered unfair business practices, though corporations, of course, could challenge FTC rulings in the courts. Soon after, Wilson got Congress to pass the Clayton Antitrust Act, which increased the strength and reach of the Sherman Antitrust Act. For example, it disallowed "interlocking directorates," in which a lot of the same people sat on the boards of different companies in the same, or related, industries, where they might create virtual monopolies.

Taken together, the new agencies set up to handle the new regulations on business, "virtually constituted a new branch of government," says one historian. They were a significant step away from the old laissez-faire principle by which American government had operated for a century.

By the election year of 1916, war was going on in Europe, and Wilson was preoccupied with it. He won reelection on the slogan, "He kept us out of the war." Although the war took up more and more of his energy, he continued to press for progressive measures, like the Federal Farm Loan Act, which helped farmers with long-term financing of their farms. In April 1917, the United States joined World War I. (United States

PUT STRENGTH IN THE FINAL BLOW BUY WAR BONDS

In April 1917 the United States entered World War I. By that time the war was taking up much of President Wilson's energy, and he had less time to fight for progressive measures.

involvement in World War I is described in the volume in this series called *The United States Enters the World Stage*.) The war was over in November 1918, but for a year thereafter Wilson was totally involved with negotiating the peace, and fighting to get it ratified by the Senate. The Senate turned down most of what Wilson wanted. In the struggle Wilson became ill and no longer had the strength to fight for progressive measures. When he left office in 1920 the progressive movement appeared to be finished—although, as we shall see, it was only temporarily on hold.

American political progressivism lasted for twenty years. It accomplished much by way of legislation, but in truth, the net effect on those it was supposed to benefit was small. Although there were some improvements, farmers, laborers, and the poor were still not getting anything like their fair share of the nation's wealth. Progressive policies would only come into their own in the 1930s, when the Great Depression forced Americans to rethink a great many things, as we shall see.

CHAPTER III

The Roaring Twenties

The decade of the 1920s in America has always been portrayed in books and movies as a prosperous time, with the stock market steadily rising, new ideas and types of art sprouting everywhere, and the American people flinging off tired old ways to live new, exciting lives. And some of this is true. But there was another side to the 1920s that was not so glamorous, for the prosperity was not equally spread, and certain groups, like African-Americans, were not invited to the party at all.

Let us look at the happy side first. Between 1919 and 1928, the average of all incomes rose a third—though much of this went to the already well-off. New technologies were making lives for most people easier. For example, in 1912 only one-sixth of American homes were wired for electricity; most people still used candles, and oil and gas lamps. By 1927 two-thirds of American homes had wiring, bringing with it electric stoves, toasters, vacuum cleaners, fans, clothes washing machines, and other appliances.

Electricity hastened the spread of a new invention, radio. The first commercial broadcast was made in 1920; by 1924 there were five hun-

In the 1920s many technological innovations changed American lives. The first commercial radio broadcast was made in 1920. Very quickly radios went into millions of homes, bringing cheap entertainment to ordinary people.

dred commercial stations, and by 1929 two-fifths of American homes had radios. Housewives not only had electric irons, washing machines, and vacuum cleaners to ease their labor, but music from the radio to ease the tedium of work.

Even more significant was the coming of the automobile: Hardly any invention changed American life as much as did the car. Made practical only in the 1890s, by 1910 the automobile was still mostly a plaything for the rich, frequently breaking down, and capable of going only twenty or thirty miles an hour. Over the next few years, Henry Ford and his imitators drove prices down. Ford's Model T, perhaps the most celebrated of all cars, was sold to ordinary people in the millions. Closed "sedans" began to be widely used after 1923, making driving more comfortable. In 1915 there were 2.5 million cars in the United States; by 1920 it was 9 million and by 1925, 20 million.

As more people bought cars, they put pressure on politicians to pave the dirt roads that existed everywhere, and to build new "parkways." As

Even more dramatic changes were brought by the arrival of the inexpensive automobile. The 1917 Willys-Overland (at left) was chauffeur driven, and was an expensive car for the wealthy. At right, a busy street in Washington, D.C., in 1928 shows inexpensive enclosed sedans, which even working people could afford.

roads improved—with a vast expenditure of state and local income tax— more people were encouraged to buy cars. Gas stations, billboards, hot dog stands, tourist cabins followed. As it became possible to drive ever longer distances conveniently, new suburbs grew around central cities. The older suburbs had been built along trolley and railroad lines and had to be small enough so commuters could walk to the stations. With cars, a suburban community could be built anywhere, and they began to grow at considerable distances from the cities. People could now visit friends and relatives they had formerly seen only infrequently. Vacation trips— for those who had vacations—to mountains and seashores were easier. American life was permanently altered by the automobile in the 1920s.

The Strange Case of Prohibition

There have always been those who think that people ought to drink alcohol only in moderation or not at all. Many Americans had long been concerned with what they saw as the social problems caused by alcoholism. Over the years crusades had been mounted to control drinking—or ban it outright. For the most part, they never got very far.

However, through the last decade of the 1800s, the clamor for the prohibition of alcoholic beverages grew. It was believed that too many men were drinking up their wages Saturday night, leaving their families to go hungry. Employers believed that a sober worker was a good worker. Alcohol caused crime, others said; other commentators pointed to alcohol-related family violence. Gradually, laws limiting the sale of alcohol were passed in some towns, counties, and even states.

The "wets" fought back against the "drys." The wets were strong in the big cities, where, among other things, there were immigrant groups who included alcohol in their cultures: Italians customarily drank wine with their meals, Germans had always had their beer gardens, Irish had the tradition of the saloon. Nonetheless, public opinion was turning against alcohol consumption.

With the start of World War I, it was said that the nation ought not to waste resources like rye, barley, and corn in making alcohol; besides, citizens ought to be clearheaded for the task ahead. By 1917 nineteen states prohibited the sale and/or manufacture of alcohol. Soon a constitutional amendment barring the manufacture and sale of alcohol was passed, and on January 16, 1920, the United States went dry.

Or was supposed to. In fact, it did not. Liquor was smuggled in from Canada or brought by fast small boats from ships anchored behind the twelve-mile limit. Millions of gallons of medicinal alcohol were converted to the drinkable kind. Americans made their own beer and gin at home, giving rise to the term "bathtub gin." Saloons were replaced by illegal bars set up in private homes and apartment cellars, called "speakeasies." Since the sale of alcohol was illegal, accurate statistics on consumption are very hard to develop. Whether alcohol consumption actually declined is not known for sure, but most historians think it did.

Perhaps the worst aspect of prohibition is that the liquor industry came to be controlled by gangsters. There were bloody gang wars, with innocent bystanders sometimes killed. The government tried to enforce Prohibition, but by the mid-twenties public opinion had swung around and the majority of Americans did not want it enforced. To many Americans, imbued with the new spirit of freedom and expressiveness, breaking the liquor laws seemed like a praiseworthy act of defiance. The government enforcement agency was undermanned and underfunded, and there was no strong pressure to make enforcement work. By the end of the 1920s the majority of Americans believed that Prohibition had failed. When a new government took office in 1933, a repeal amendment was submitted to the states and was quickly ratified. Prohibition was the nation's most glaring failure to control private behavior.

Perhaps even more important than technical improvements was a change in American attitudes and ways of thinking. From about 1830 to World War I, America, and much of the Western world, had been dominated by what is known as Victorianism, named for the queen of England who reigned much of that time. Like all such things, Victorianism was complex. Put simply, it upheld the idea of putting duty, honor, and your family and community ahead of yourself. People should also be frugal. The Victorians believed in order and decency. They did not like wild emotional excesses, but thought that people ought to be mannerly and considerate of others. Not everybody could live up to this ideal, but most people tried.

However, in time the Victorian ideal was exaggerated in some—mostly religious—groups who seemed to believe that any kind of fun or enjoyment was wrong. You weren't supposed to drink even in moderation, should only dance very sedately, should not even mention sex. Inevitably, people chafed under these restrictions. By the 1890s novelists like Theodore Dreiser and Stephen Crane were writing about sex, drinking, and more emotional ways of behaving. Philosophers and psychologists like John Dewey, William James, and Sigmund Freud began saying that the free expression of feelings was not necessarily bad. Artists began painting scenes of ordinary life, indeed slum life. Very quickly there grew up the idea that people ought to live free and expressive lives instead of repressive ones, sternly doing their duty and behaving decorously. By 1915 these new ideas were being widely discussed by artists, writers, and intellectuals in places like New York's Greenwich Village, where such people congregated. These ideas would permit people greater freedom than allowed under Victorian attitudes. The ideas spread, and during the 1920s they became the basis for the spirit of the age.

Many people fought against the new ideas. It was mainly the young who took them up. Young people came to believe that not only *could* they go out dancing, drinking, and having parties, but that they *should*

In the 1910s the old Victorian ethic still lingered; no well-brought-up young woman would consider showing her legs in public; dresses reached to the ankles. By 1929, as in the picture at right, dresses were up to the knee, and frequently above. This dramatic shift in dress styles reflected a new attitude toward morals and having fun in general.

spend as much time as possible having fun. Inevitably, rates for divorce, for alcohol abuse, and for sex before marriage climbed.

One group that benefited greatly from the new attitude was women. Women began increasingly to insist upon the right to smoke, to drink in speakeasies, to cut their hair short and wear revealing clothes. By 1919 women had won the right to vote in fifteen states and in thirteen more they could vote in presidential elections. Not surprisingly, the Nineteenth Amendment, guaranteeing women the right to vote everywhere was ratified in 1920. Although women did make progress in finding careers, most women still had to work at home as wives and mothers. An abun-

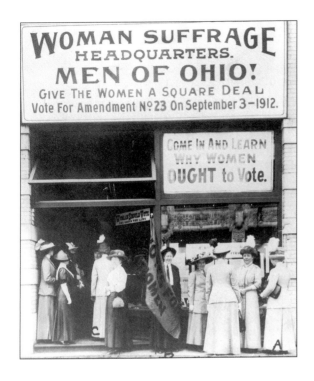

More significantly, it was also the time when women finally got the vote, after many years of struggle: Again and again, efforts to pass women's suffrage measures were defeated, until new attitudes took over after World War I.

dance of other women served them as maids and cooks. But both groups benefited greatly from all the new electrical appliances.

There was much about the 1920s that was an improvement over earlier times, and many people began to live easier, less restricted, lives. But not everybody benefited: In fact, probably a majority of Americans were only slightly better off in the 1920s than they had been before World War I; and some were worse off.

To begin with, while wages for ordinary workers did rise somewhat on average, a great many did not share the prosperity. People were shifting from coal to oil for home heating. Additionally, new mining techniques were eliminating many jobs. There was much unemployment and outright poverty in coal-mining areas like Appalachia in Kentucky. Similarly, the use of synthetic fibers in cloth hurt the cotton industry. So did the much less full clothing styles of the 1920s, which reduced the amount of cloth used in dresses by half. Unemployment rose in the textile industry. And despite some of the benefits progressive measures had brought to workers, they and their families still had hard lives, always scrambling to find enough money, not for luxuries, but for basic necessities like food, clothing, and their small apartments.

Farmers, too, failed to gain much from the prosperity of the 1920s. It was the same old problem for them: too much wheat, corn, beef, and cotton in the fields, the warehouses, and the grain elevators, forcing prices down, while prices for the things farmers had to buy were high and rising. Prices for fertilizer and farm equipment rose. Prices for farm produce fell as the war ended: Between 1919 and 1921, corn went from $1.52 to 52 cents a bushel; wheat from $2.16 to $1.03. Farm debt rose from $6.3 billion in 1914 to $14.1 billion in 1921. More than eight thousand families who owned their own farms in 1910 were tenants paying rent by 1930.

African-Americans—about 10 percent of the population—were even worse off. In the years from about 1890 to 1910, white southerners had made great efforts to push blacks back into a serfdom much like the slavery they had escaped after the Civil War. Laws were passed making it

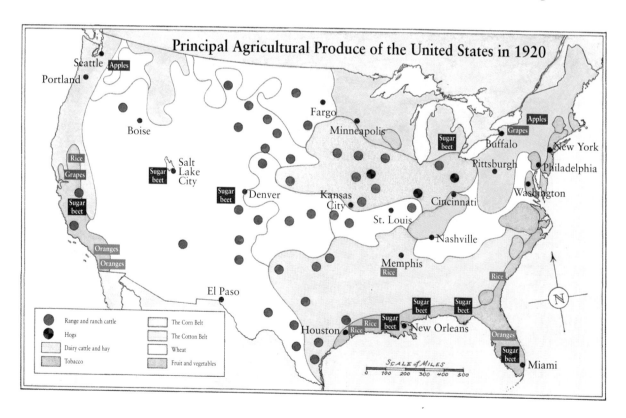

Principal Agricultural Produce of the United States in 1920

impossible for African-American citizens to vote. Many blacks were lynched, which intimidated others so they wouldn't demand equal treatment or other rights. Then, particularly during World War I, when there were plenty of jobs in northern factories, blacks migrated by the millions to New York, Chicago, Philadelphia, Washington, D.C., and elsewhere, hoping to find better pay and freer lives than they had in the South. Life for many African-Americans improved. Still, in the 1920s they were generally the worst paid of all workers, "last hired, first fired," and in the cities mainly lived in squalid slums.

Economically, then, the decade of the 1920s was by no means a time of universal prosperity: Some people gained; some people lost. Socially and politically there were pluses and minuses as well. While it is true that women gained some freedoms they had not enjoyed before, and people in general were less restricted than they had been by the old Victorian morality, there were also some counterbalancing restrictive tendencies.

For one, there arose a belief by many government officials, and much of the general public as well, that a Communist conspiracy represented a real threat to the American way of life. Hundreds of people—many of them foreign born—were

Lynching remained a horrible fact of life through the 1920s. These two men were accused of murder, but before they could be tried, they were taken from the jail and lynched.

unconstitutionally jailed or forcibly sent out of the country because they held, or were thought to hold, unpopular opinions. This widespread, but short-lived panic of 1919-1920 has been called a "Red Scare" because of the association of the word Reds with Communists. Another setback for free speech and academic freedom came in 1925, when several states banned the teaching of Charles Darwin's evolutionary theory of human development. A public school science teacher in Tennessee, John Scopes, was found guilty of doing so in a trial that pitted science against certain religious beliefs.

Then, the great wave of immigration that peaked in the years just after 1900 troubled many Americans who did not like to see "strange" people with "strange" ways in their midst. Immigrants were sometimes physically attacked. Finally, in 1924, Congress enacted laws—the first such laws in American history—that restricted how many immigrants could come to the United States each year. The quotas heavily favored people from the nations of Northern Europe like England, Ireland, and Germany and worked against Southern and Eastern Europeans from such places as Italy and Poland. Foreigners were also often the target of the Ku Klux Klan, an anti-black, anti-Catholic, anti-Semitic group that had been organized in the South after the Civil War to oppress African-Americans. It found thousands of enthusiastic members all across the nation in a revival of interest and influence during the 1920s.

The 1920s, then, had both good and bad sides. The main gainers from twenties prosperity were the very rich, who had the money to benefit from large investments, and the urban middle class, who could afford the new labor-saving devices, automobiles, and suburban houses that were changing America. Other groups did see some improvement to their lives, but it was not great. The large pockets of poverty among farmers, textile workers, miners, and African-Americans significantly undercut the apparent prosperity. It was these—and, as we shall see, other—underlying weaknesses in the economy that led to the Depression of the 1930s.

CHAPTER IV

The Incredible Bull Market
of the 1920s

If anything characterized the 1920s it was the roaring, surging Bull Market that brought prices for stocks to unbelievable levels for that time. It was driven by the optimistic spirit that a new America was aborning, and that everybody could be rich. And when it collapsed, it set off the Great Depression.

Let's take a look at how the stock market works. To explain briefly, some companies are "privately held," which means that they are owned by a person, a family, or a small group of people. Privately held companies are not involved in the stock market. Other companies are "publicly held," with their stocks bought and sold on one of various stock markets by private individuals and "institutional investors" like big pension plans and insurance companies. A stock is a share in a company that may have been issued when the company was first organized, or at some later time, as when a privately held company "goes public." If the company makes a profit, it is distributed according to how many shares each person owns. People buy shares of stocks to get this regular "dividend" income. Of course if the company does not make a profit there may be no dividends.

A share of stock indicates ownership of a certain portion of a company. This is a certificate for shares in the Great Southern Coal and Iron Company.

The real value of a stock, then, has something to do with the size of the dividends it pays. The value of a stock normally depends upon the dividends it is likely to pay in forthcoming years, and while a company that has paid good dividends in the past is likely to go on paying them, there is no guarantee of it. A technological improvement, for example, can hurt a whole industry, as when oil heat began to replace coal.

But not all people buy stocks for their dividends. Many people simply speculate in stocks, in essence betting on which ones will increase in price, and which will decrease. The speculators don't care about the true *value* of a stock, only the *price* of it. If a lot of people think that a stock will go up they will buy it, in the process bidding the price up. Sometimes stock prices get bid up to wholly unreal levels having nothing to do with any sensible estimate of their value. Of course speculators know that the stock can fall, too; they hope they will be smart enough to sell before the stock breaks.

This is what happened during the Great Bull Market of the 1920s. In about 1923, the economy appeared to be growing, and stock prices began, reasonably, to rise. Soon people began to see that if you bought five shares of General Motors stock at $200 ($1,000) and the next day it went to $220, you would have earned $100 overnight.

But the game was even better than that. Through a broker, you could buy on *margin*—that is to say, put up as little as 10 percent. In such a case you could buy your $1,000 worth of General Motors stock for $100, and your profit would still be $100, or 100 percent—overnight.

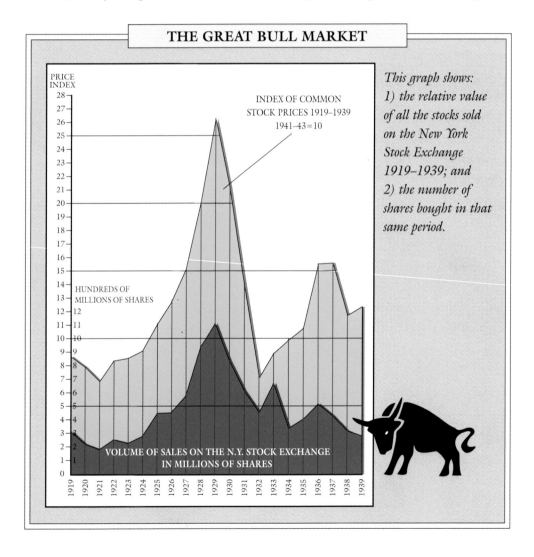

THE GREAT BULL MARKET

PRICE INDEX

INDEX OF COMMON STOCK PRICES 1919–1939 1941–43=10

HUNDREDS OF MILLIONS OF SHARES

VOLUME OF SALES ON THE N.Y. STOCK EXCHANGE IN MILLIONS OF SHARES

This graph shows: 1) the relative value of all the stocks sold on the New York Stock Exchange 1919–1939; and 2) the number of shares bought in that same period.

As more and more people saw this, they jumped into the stock market—not just wealthy investors but a lot of ordinary people betting a few hundred dollars of hard-earned savings that the stock market would go up.

Inevitably, with everybody buying, the market did go up, up, up. By 1928 the stock market had reached a height that had many speculators looking nervously over their shoulders. Surely it would break soon. And indeed there were a few sharp breaks that hurt some small speculators and investors. But each time, the market recovered and went roaring on up.

There were signs that all was not well: American business was slowing down and unemployment was growing. And, as we have seen, there were those troubling soft spots in farming, textiles, coal. The speculators paid no attention. In the beginning of March 1928, General Motors was at 139¾. Soon it was over 150. On into 1929 the Bull Market roared. American Can, which had been at 77 in March 1929, was over 180 by September; Radio Corporation leaped from 120 to 160 in a single day; and other stocks did likewise. In September and October, the stock market wavered; some stockholders grew more nervous, but others kept plunging ahead. On October 23 the market experienced another sharp break, and the next day the whole edifice collapsed. Thursday, October 24, is still remembered as Black Thursday on Wall Street.

As the downward slide grew worse that terrible day, investors began to panic, and tried to sell all the stocks they owned at whatever price they could get. This drove prices down even faster: In two hours General Motors went from 205½ to 193½; General Electric went from 315 to 283. The market steadied for a day or two, but Tuesday, October 29, was even worse than Black Thursday: The popular White Sewing Machine stock, which had been at 48, had fallen to 11.

The panic then eased a little, and the fall slowed. But despite ups and downs, the stock market continued to fall irregularly but surely. By November, many stocks had lost half their value and some had lost two-thirds.

Black Thursday: A crowd gathers to read news of plummeting stock prices.

The stock market crash had a widening effect, poisoning everything it touched. Many banks had been speculating in the stock market with their depositors' money instead of lending it to businesses and home owners as they had before. When the market collapsed, American banks lost billions and many closed up, leaving people who had their money in them standing sadly before locked doors, their savings gone.

What caused the stock market crash of 1929? Obviously, overoptimism, the belief that stock prices would always go up, was a principal cause. Buying on margin—that is, with borrowed money—meant that speculators would have to sell quickly when the stock they owned no longer was worth as much as they owed their stockbrokers. But perhaps the most fundamental cause of the crash was that the underlying economy was weak and getting weaker and prices of shares in corporations did not reflect their real value.

The next question, then, is why did the crash lead to a decade-long depression? After all, there had been crashes before followed by quick recovery of both the market and the overall economy. Some economists think that the depression—or something like it—would have occurred

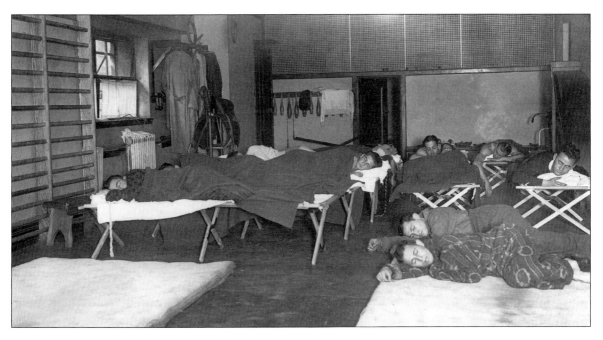

In the terrible last week of October so many shares of stock were sold that clerks had to work all night to keep up. Here some of them catch up on their sleep in a gym near the Wall Street area.

even if there had been no crash on the stock market. There were long-term problems of over-production, reduced sales in foreign markets because of our high protective tariffs, and, as we have seen, substantial weaknesses in agriculture, coal, and textiles. Something else only the shrewdest investors noticed: In 1927, the construction of new houses fell off dramatically, foretelling a wide decline in the economy overall. No new houses meant no new refrigerators, carpets, vacuum cleaners, tables, chairs, and all the rest.

But there is a fairly general agreement among historians and economists that a basic cause of the Depression of the 1930s was maldistribution of income due in large measure to the fact that wages for too many Americans were falling behind. Labor productivity was up by 43 percent:

That is, modern methods and machines allowed each worker to produce much more than before. But by 1929, wages for factory workers had gone up only 8 percent—some economists say much less. The difference was being pocketed by the rich and the middle class. To give just one figure, in 1923 the richest 5 percent of Americans took 22.9 percent of the income; by 1929 it was 30 percent. The poorest 40 percent of families had only 12 percent of the income.

The net effect was that by 1929 or so every family that could afford to buy a car or radio already had one. The rest could not afford them, so that millions of workers could not buy the very goods that they were turning out. When people could not buy, companies could not sell. They reduced production and laid off workers, creating a downward spiral. By 1931 the economy had fallen 28 percent—that is, the great American industrial machine was producing that much less of everything, employing that many fewer workers, and showing little or no profit at all. The country was now pitched into an economic swamp that would blight the lives of millions, and from which some people would never recover.

CHAPTER V

The Hardest Times

It is very difficult for people today to understand how bad the Great Depression was. It hit the nation like a giant hammer, sending cracks through the whole structure. In March 1930 somewhere between 3 million and 4 million people were out of work. By March 1931 the number of unemployed had doubled to 8 million. A year later it was up to about 12 million and by March 1933 the number was between 14 and 16 million—and this was in a nation with much less than half the population it had in 2000.

But even those who had jobs suffered. Many factories were operating only two or three days a week and paying workers who had not been well-off during good times half what they had earned before. Manufacturers tried to keep wages up, fearing wage cuts would reduce demand for their products even more, but inevitably wages began to slide. Average weekly wages went from $28.50 in 1929 to $25.74 the year after that.

We must remember that there was no unemployment insurance in those days and not much welfare of any kind. Towns and cities tried to help their unemployed the best way they could, but tax collections were down and there was not much they could do. In Philadelphia "relief" payments were $4.39 a *week* for a family. Prices were much lower then; even so, a family could not even begin to feed itself on that small an amount.

So people went hungry. The mother might mix flour and water and bake it to make a kind of bread. Other families would cut back to two meals a day, a breakfast of cocoa, bread and butter at 11 A.M., supper in the late afternoon of canned soup. Many families ate nothing but potatoes, rice, bread, and coffee. Others bought stale bread for three cents a loaf. Some begged unsold fish or vegetables from shops at the end of the day. At times people went without any food at

Perhaps the most famous photograph to come out of the Depression, this picture by Dorothea Lange shows a migrant mother and her children staring into a dismal future. Lange and other photographers were hired by various government agencies to record the misery of the Depression, and to give photographers jobs.

all for a day or two. Not many actually starved to death, but there were plenty of cases where they came close. Skinny, hollow-eyed children could be seen everywhere.

Of course, between two-thirds and three-quarters of American workers still had jobs; many had not taken pay cuts, and some people actually got raises during the Depression. But it was also probably true that almost every American family had a member who was out of work—a son, an aunt, or a brother, and these people had to be helped, perhaps even taken into the home. Millions saw nothing in their futures but more tough times, and almost everybody lived with the fear that they, too, could lose their jobs. The population of cities actually fell as people

Working people had seen hard times before, but the Depression came as a great shock to the middle class. This man had bought stock on margin, and when the market collapsed had to sell his possessions to pay his debts.

moved back to live with family members in the countryside, where they could grow vegetables and keep hens.

The Depression came as a particular shock to the middle class, about a third of all Americans. Working people had always known periods of hard times, and African-Americans had hardly known anything else. Middle-class families may have had to pull in their horns from time to time, but they had always felt that if they worked hard and led honest, frugal lives, they would be secure.

During the Depression that sense of security evaporated. Small businesspeople, like shopkeepers and dressmakers, saw their businesses collapse. Business managers lost their jobs, lawyers lost their clients. By 1932 nearly five thousand banks had failed. Nine million depositors lost all their savings. Businesses failed and home owners faced foreclosure because they could not get their money. Millions of people with home mortgages had their houses taken from them. Their children gave up dreams of college and hunted for any jobs they could get in order to help the family. Older sons and daughters put off marriage because they could not afford to set up housekeeping on their own. Thousands of men—we remember that few middle-class women of the time worked outside of the home—who had been stockbrokers, accountants, even presidents of companies, found themselves selling newspapers or apples on street corners.

But despite the shock the Depression brought to the middle class, it was working people who suffered most. The majority of them lived on the edge of desperation, eating cheap food, always behind in the rent, scrambling at the end of the month to pay the gas and electric bills, patching their clothes, stuffing cardboard in their shoes to cover holes in their soles, shivering as they trudged the streets in winter looking for work because they could not afford a secondhand overcoat.

Farmers were just as badly off. They had seen hard times all through the 1920s, and now things were even worse. Prices for food fell by more than half between 1929 and 1933. Net income for farmers was down by

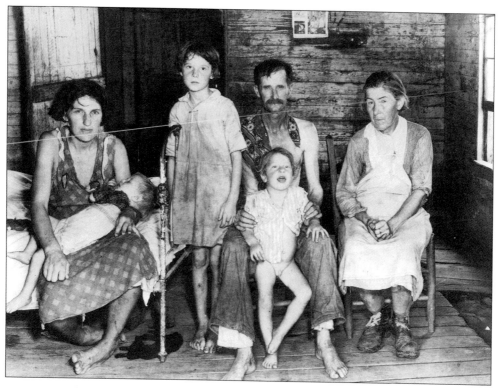

The suffering of farm families was intense. This Alabama sharecropper and his family, living in a tiny cabin, went without shoes, owned a minimum of clothes, and the most basic furniture. The photographer was Walker Evans, another of the now celebrated people who recorded the Depression for the government.

two-thirds. Many farmers had mortgages and other debts, and now could not make the payments on their loans. Something had to give. Buildings went unrepaired; farm machines grew old and weary. Some farmers could not afford fertilizer and their crops suffered. Even with economies, thousands of farmers lost their farms because they could not pay on their loans: In 1929 about 2 percent of farms were foreclosed on; by 1932 this figure had more than doubled. This was despite the fact that sympathetic farm area bankers and local officials did their best not to foreclose. Realistically, to whom would a bank sell a farm it had taken over?

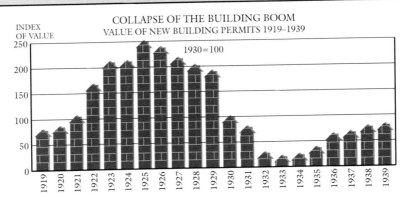

COLLAPSE OF THE BUILDING BOOM
VALUE OF NEW BUILDING PERMITS 1919–1939

1930 = 100

The building boom crashed after 1929, but note that it began to slide in 1926

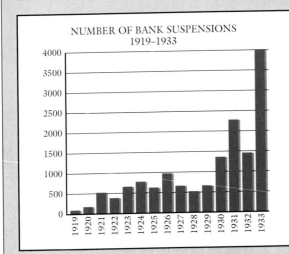

NUMBER OF BANK SUSPENSIONS
1919–1933

The number of banks that had to stop doing business (often temporarily) peaked in 1933, causing President Roosevelt to shut down all banks for at least a few days. But note the number of suspensions in 1926.

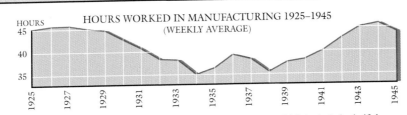

HOURS WORKED IN MANUFACTURING 1925–1945
(WEEKLY AVERAGE)

Note that it was customary to work forty-five hours a week—which included a half day on Saturday—until the Depression. When manufacturers began to get military contracts, starting about 1938, the work week began to get longer until, in 1943, a full forty-five hour week became normal again.

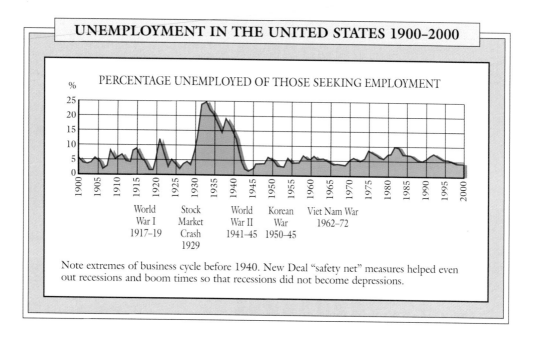

UNEMPLOYMENT IN THE UNITED STATES 1900–2000

PERCENTAGE UNEMPLOYED OF THOSE SEEKING EMPLOYMENT

World
War I
1917–19

Stock
Market
Crash
1929

World
War II
1941–45

Korean
War
1950–45

Viet Nam War
1962–72

Note extremes of business cycle before 1940. New Deal "safety net" measures helped even out recessions and boom times so that recessions did not become depressions.

On top of everything, nature struck at the farmers, too. In 1930, just as the Depression began, much of the eastern part of the United States was hit by a long, severe drought. In 1931 the center of the drought shifted to the Great Plains: Much of Montana and the Dakotas was as dry as a desert. Between 1930 and 1936 almost every state in the nation suffered from periods of drought, but the Great Plains area was the hardest hit.

Making matters worse, farmers on the Great Plains often used soil-destroying methods of cultivation. They planted the same crop year after year, which impoverished the soil, and they plowed in such a way that the topsoil would wash off during a rain, leaving gulches and gullies. Such methods, combined with drought, produced mammoth dust storms. In May 1934 high winds in Montana and Wyoming picked up dirt from the ground and swirled it aloft, until 350 million tons of dust were being carried in the air. The storm went eastward to Chicago, where it dumped four pounds of dust onto the city for each inhabitant. It went on to the

Oklahoma and surrounding states, ripped by drought and dust storms, became known as the Dust Bowl. Millions of acres were no longer fertile, and farmers abandoned the farms to head westward in hope of jobs on California fruit and vegetable farms.

east coast cities and out to sea: Ships three hundred miles off the coast found light coatings of dust on their decks.

There were many such dust storms. People caught outdoors might not be able to see a foot in front of them: Seal doors and windows, and still the dust blew in, covering furniture, clothes, the baby in the cradle. With the dust storms went the topsoil, ruining the farmland.

Farmers began to flee the Great Plains. The story of the migrant "Okies" from Oklahoma has been told with great drama by John Steinbeck in his classic novel, *The Grapes of Wrath*. Tens of thousands of families from the Dust Bowl states lost their money, their farms, sold everything they had for what they could get. They packed their children, pitiful parcels of clothes, a favorite chair or two in old, worn automobiles and headed westward for California, where there were supposed to be good jobs. But there were never enough jobs for the thousands going westward. Wages dropped to rock bottom. Thousands of people ended up living in the notorious migrant-worker camps, where whole families lived in tents, sharing rough toilets, eating poor food, and bathing in ditches.

This, then, was the human face of the Depression. Not everybody suffered: Schoolteachers, for example, usually kept their jobs, although they might take pay cuts or even go without pay at times. The entertainment business, driven by radio, the new talking films, the vogue for "swing" dance bands, was strong. But most industries stagnated, or even sank. The great majority of American families suffered to one degree or another, and many lived at the edge of desperation year after year. All anyone could ask was, would it ever end?

A group of "Okies" heading for California in an automobile as worn and weary as the people it carries.

CHAPTER VI

The Hundred Days

In 1920 the American people were tired of wartime sacrifices and democratic crusades. They wanted instead what the new president, Warren Harding, called "normalcy," and a good time. Harding was amiable and handsome, but lacked the qualities necessary to be president. He put into office around him old political friends. Some of them took bribes in exchange for favors and government money. By 1923 the scandals were leaking out and Harding suddenly died. It was rumored that he had committed suicide, or even had been murdered, but there is no evidence for either.

Vice President Calvin Coolidge took over. He was a silent, unimaginative man who did as little as possible to disturb the seeming prosperity of the 1920s. His successor, Herbert Hoover, was quite a different sort. By training an engineer, he had become well known for successfully managing food relief organizations during World War I. In 1921 he became secretary of commerce. Hoover was intelligent and a good organizer. Unfortunately for him, he took office only a few months before the 1929 stock market crash.

Hoover has often been thought of as a president who sat on his hands *(right)* Warren G. Harding looked every inch a president, and in 1920 promised Americans just what they wanted, a return to "normalcy" after the sacrifices of the war years. But he proved to be weak and incompetent.

(below) Calvin Coolidge (at left) with his wife on the way to his inauguration. Coolidge was competent enough, but wished to rock no boats and did as little as possible.

while the country rolled into the Depression, but in fact he tried hard to revive the economy, without, however, abandoning laissez-faire. He exhorted businessmen not to cut wages, not to lay people off. He asked them to take little or no profits, asked unions not to demand pay increases. Eventually he got Congress to set up the Reconstruction Finance Corporation to make emergency loans to banks, railroads, and other groups—but only those with the likelihood of paying back the loans.

In his heart Hoover believed in laissez-faire, that government should not play a large role in the economy. His main idea was to get corporations, unions, and workers to do voluntarily what was necessary to revive the economy. He did not want simply to hand out money to the unemployed, no matter how hard-pressed they were. He advocated a "trickle down" theory: If he could help banks and large corporations get going again, the benefits would trickle down to everybody. Thus, while Hoover did try things, nothing he did had much effect because he would not give up on laissez-faire. In 1932, unsurprisingly, the voters turned to the Democrats, electing one of the

Herbert Hoover was a dynamic man who had the misfortune to take the presidency just before the stock market crash of 1929. He tried hard to end the Depression, but believed in laissez-faire and would not take strong enough measures.

most dynamic presidents the nation has ever had, Franklin Delano Roosevelt. The Democrats also took over Congress, so that Roosevelt had a good chance to get his programs through.

It is generally believed that a new president has a "honeymoon" during his first months in office when the public and Congress will give his plans a chance. It is certainly the case that during the first hundred days of the Roosevelt administration a vast quantity of sweeping new legislation went through. The period has come to be known as Roosevelt's Hundred Days.

Franklin Roosevelt had been born into a very wealthy family with a large estate on the Hudson River north of New York City. He was educated at home until he was a teenager, then went to private school and Harvard University. Eventually he entered politics, becoming assistant secretary of the navy during World War I, and in 1920 he was the Democratic candidate for vice president. In 1921 he was struck down with polio, which left him crippled, unable to walk without help even with the use of braces and canes. Despite this misfortune, in 1928 he was elected governor of New York, where he became the most active of all the governors in attempting to help people weather the Depression. By 1932 a well-known national figure, he got the Democratic nomination for president and won easily.

It is odd that this wealthy member of the upper class should be remembered as a fighter for the underdog. Early experience handling "small claims" court lawsuits for ordinary people gave him some idea of what workers were up against. His wife, Eleanor, to be a major influence in the America of her time, was also important in awakening his sympathy for working people. No doubt his illness helped him to identify with people who had had bad luck. In any case, he early on spoke for the "forgotten man at the bottom of the economic pyramid." Like everybody else, he was struck by the paradox of a nation in which millions were going hungry while farmers were suffering from a glut of food. In his first speech as a presidential candidate, he said, "I pledge you, I pledge myself, to a new deal for the American people." A journalist picked up the phrase "new deal," and Roosevelt's administration has been known as the New Deal ever since.

In his inaugural address Roosevelt told the nation, "We have nothing to fear but fear itself—nameless, unreasoning, unjustified terror which paralyzes needed efforts to convert retreat into advance." These lines became famous. However, as Roosevelt knew, there was more wrong with the economy than fear, and he followed his words with bold action.

Roosevelt was by no means a radical. Nevertheless, he was willing to try new and different schemes. Neither the conservatives on the right, nor the people on the left, liked Roosevelt's position. The left wing wanted to see the government *nationalize* many industries, like railroads, steel, oil, and especially the banks. That is, the government would simply take over these businesses, own them and run them. The conservatives, on the other hand, as usual, favored laissez-faire, with the government staying out of business as much as possible. Roosevelt took a middle road: He wanted to save the capitalist system, but he also wanted it limited and controlled in various ways by government so that it would work for the good of everybody, the workers as well as owners and managers.

Historians have generally divided New Deal measures into three groups: *relief, recovery,* and *reform.* Relief was simply immediate aid to the worst sufferers. Recovery measures were meant to get the economy going again. Reform programs were intended to be permanent. In fact, a lot of the supposedly temporary measures also proved to be permanent, as we shall see.

The first move of the new Roosevelt administration was to help the banks out of trouble. As we have seen, many banks had been speculating in stocks, and had closed their doors when the stock market had crashed. Of course, millions of people started to draw their money out of other banks just to be safe. Banks do not have on hand all the money people have deposited in them. They have lent most of it out to businesses or people who want to buy houses, cars, and so forth. When a lot of people suddenly want to take their money of the bank, the bank may not have enough, and perfectly sound banks can get into trouble when there is a "run" on them like this.

By early 1933, before the new government came in, many states had begun to shut down their banks for a few days at a time when they were threatened by runs. The first thing Roosevelt did after his inauguration was to declare a four-day nationwide bank "holiday," along with other banking measures. It was a strange moment for the country, when most people, even those well-off, had no cash to pay for simple things, like a cup of coffee, a ride in the subway. Many stores let people charge for whatever they needed, and some cities and states even issued "scrip," that is, a temporary substitute for money that could be turned in for real dollars when the crisis was over.

Government accountants were sent in to inspect banks' books, and banks that proved to be sound were quickly reopened. Public confidence in banks rose, and the private banking system was saved. Later in the Hundred Days other bank reforms were put in. The most important of these was the Glass-Steagall Banking Act. This act, among other measures, set up controls to prevent banks from using savings deposits to invest in the stock market. It also created the Federal Deposit Insurance Corporation (FDIC), which insured people's bank accounts for up to $5,000. (This sum was raised from time to time and was $100,000 in 2000.)

Roosevelt then turned his attention to the economy in general. Herbert Hoover had believed that the way to get things going again was to give money to businesses so they could hire workers. Roosevelt decided that there was no point in keeping businesses going if nobody had money to buy their products. He believed that the best idea would be to get money into the hands of consumers, who could then buy, and get businesses selling and manufacturers producing again.

One of his first attempts to do this was the famous Civilian Conservation Corps, known as the CCC, which employed men between the ages of eighteen and twenty-five to plant trees, build new parks, and do other useful tasks. Eventually 2 million young men (no women) worked for the CCC. At the same time the government set up the Civil Works Administration to give money to states and municipalities for construction projects that could put many people to work very quickly.

An even more important agency was the Public Works Administration, known as the

Young men in the CCC were put to work at many types of jobs. Here a group of them are planting Douglas fir seedlings to reforest a burned-over area. The CCC was a semi-military organization, in which the men often lived in barracks and ate in mess halls, as soldiers did.

PWA. This program spent millions of dollars to put people to work building roads, post offices, schools, and much else. In time the PWA spent over $4 billion for 34,000 projects. Today many American students go to schools and play in playgrounds built by the PWA.

Of particular importance to Roosevelt was the plight of the farmers: About a quarter of all Americans belonged to farm families and, as we have seen, most of them had been suffering from low agriculture prices, high railroad rates, drought, and dust storms for nearly fifteen years. By the time Roosevelt took office, the nation's agriculture was on the edge of catastrophe.

Very quickly the government expanded Hoover's program that offered farmers inexpensive loans and mortgages so their farms would not be taken over by the banks. Another scheme

The PWA built thousands of roads, bridges, post offices, schools, playgrounds, and much more, some of which are still in use. Here are some teenagers in Carbon Hill, Alabama, enjoy the first swimming pool the town ever had, built by the PWA.

was to try to raise farm prices by reducing the agricultural glut. Farmers were paid to let portions of their land lie idle; or, alternatively, the government would keep prices up by buying surplus crops at a set minimum price and storing them. Then, in theory, when the price rose to a certain figure, the government would sell what was stored. This was a system called "the ever normal granary" by the old progressives who first proposed it. As a result, for example, 10 million acres of cotton fields were left unplanted, reducing the cotton crop in 1933 by 4 millions bales. Cotton prices went from 5.5 cents a pound to 9.9 cents. The story was the same for wheat, corn, and many other crops. In the end, between these and other programs, farm incomes went from $5.5 billion in 1932 to $8.7 billion in 1935.

The WPA employed a wide variety of people, including writers who wrote a celebrated series on the American states, actors who put on free plays for the poor, and painters who painted murals on walls in WPA buildings, like schools and post offices. This typical WPA mural, by artist Gordon Langdon, shows a scene from working life, as many such murals did.

Central to Roosevelt's effort to get the economy going again was his determination to put commerce and industry back on its feet. The plan his advisers came up with was the National Industrial Recovery Act, or NIRA. This was a huge, complex and very sweeping program which, among other things, allowed the companies in a given industry to join together to set minimum wages and maximum hours, rule on child labor practices, set standards, specify the quality of material used and other elements of the industrial system. Some of these provisions permitted supposedly competing companies to get together in ways that would seem to violate the Sherman Antitrust Act. For instance, they could agree on a minimum price below which they promised not to go, thus curbing competition—the major regulating mechanism of free enterprise. Quickly, virtually every industry adopted codes intended to help factories stay open and keep workers on the payroll. But it was very difficult to enforce these codes and violations went uncorrected. There were other flaws, as well, and ultimately, as we shall see, parts of the NIRA were declared unconstitutional. But in the short run it had modest success, and it included some reform measures that have been permanent.

One of the most famous, and successful, programs begun during the Hundred Days was the TVA, which stands for the Tennessee Valley Authority. The idea for the TVA—which combined elements of recovery and reform—also went back to the old progressive days. Roosevelt seized upon it and expanded it. The basic scheme was to build a series of dams on the Tennessee River. These dams would accomplish many things. For one, they would create artificial lakes that in turn could be used to drive huge electric generators. In those days many rural people did not have electricity; electrifying the area would allow farmers to use power equipment, encourage industrial enterprise, and improve life generally for rural people. Controlling the rivers would also help prevent soil erosion and flooding, and irrigate dry areas. The lakes, too, could be developed for fishing, boating, and other recreational uses. Finally, the TVA would give the government a clear idea of how much it really cost to produce electricity, and thus act as a "yardstick" to be held up to private electric companies, which many thought were overcharging. The TVA turned out to be one of the most successful programs from the Hundred Days: People in the Tennessee Valley are still using electricity produced by TVA dams, which is much cheaper than electricity is in other parts of the nation.

The programs discussed here are only a sample of the many that were put in during the first Hundred Days of the Roosevelt administration. More novel and far-reaching legislation was introduced at that time than at any other since the first days of the Republic. There were programs like the Home Owners Refinancing Act, which would help people to keep their homes, and the Farm Credit Act, which aided farmers with their mortgages.

Where did the government get the money to pay for these expensive programs? Partly it was borrowed from wealthy people who managed by luck or wisdom to escape the worst of the stock market crash and were able to buy government bonds, always a very safe investment. In addition, Congress authorized the president to simply print extra money and to reduce the amount of gold and silver held in storage to back up each paper dollar.

Indeed, a lot of New Deal legislation during the Hundred Days and later concerned *monetary* policy—that is, managing the value of money. It seems strange to think of money as being "cheap" or "expensive," but that is the way economists think of it. Cheap money usually benefits working people, but reducing the amount of gold and silver backing each dollar did not raise wages and prices as hoped. (Monetarism is explained more fully in the volume in this series called *Indians, Cowboys, and Farmers and the Battle for the Great Plains.*)

Spending more money than you have is called *deficit financing*. This idea, new in the 1930s, says that in hard times the government should cut

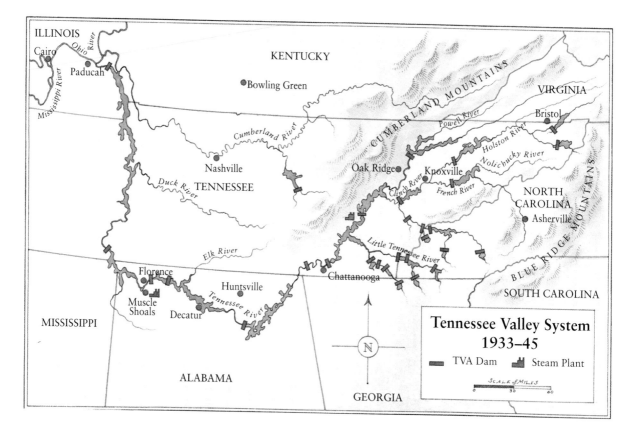

Tennessee Valley System
1933–45

TVA Dam   Steam Plant

SCALE of MILES
0   30   60

taxes and spend money, thus giving consumers more money to buy things with. In good times the government should raise taxes and cut spending. (Governments often forget this part of the theory.)

The government programs began to have some effect. Stock prices went up a little, more people found jobs, business improved, the farm crisis eased. But the improvements were small. The Depression ground on, and by 1935 it was clear that more, perhaps a lot more, had to be done.

CHAPTER VII

The Depression Rolls On

For a while after the famous Hundred Days the flood of novel measures slowed, although it hardly ceased. Then, in 1935, it picked up again. Historians have called the period 1935 to 1938 the *Second New Deal*. It began when Roosevelt made the usual State of the Union speech to Congress. He said that he had three major aims for the upcoming years: job security; security for the elderly and the ill; and slum clearance and better housing. Once again a host of new measures poured out of the White House for Congress to consider. Roosevelt was still optimistic: Things were bad, but he was sure that they could be improved if he kept trying.

However, by this time, opposition to the New Deal philosophy of active government and economic intervention was growing. Much of it came from industrialists, bankers, and corporation lawyers, who were at heart opposed to government "interference," as they termed it, in the capitalist system. These conservatives felt that many of the New Deal measures violated the Constitution. They formed a group called the Liberty League to fight Roosevelt.

There were also opponents of the New Deal with very radical ideas.

The Depression just would not quit. Demonstrators continued to march throughout the 1930s, as these women who were demanding jobs, a minimum wage of $20 a week, and unemployment compensation when they were out of work.

It was not that Roosevelt was doing too much; he was not doing enough. One of these was Charles E. Coughlin, a Catholic priest known as Father Coughlin, who had a widely heard radio program. Father Coughlin harangued millions over the air, lumping Communists, international bankers, labor unions, and the New Deal together as enemies of America. Coughlin called for radical changes in money and banking; he would have the government run all banks. Louisiana senator Huey P. Long, for a time influential, also attacked the New Deal. He demanded that the

(above) Shack towns, sometimes called "Hoovervilles," like this one in New York City's Central Park, lingered into the 1940s, when wartime employment finally made them unnecessary.

(left) Hoboes, as they were called, lived in primitive camps like this one, cooking stews and soups on rough stoves and sleeping where they could, often in doorways and under bridges.

government guarantee every American family an annual income of $2,500 a year, a very comfortable living during the Depression. His slogan, "Every man a king," attracted millions of hungry, ignorant followers. Another man who attracted attention was Francis E. Townsend of California, who wanted payments of $200 a month to everybody over sixty. Some of these schemes were foolish, but they attracted millions of voters. It was clear to Roosevelt, who wished to follow a middle road, that he had to fight both the left and right extremists.

A reform measure that did work very well, and one that continues to have great meaning for Americans today, is Social Security. It is difficult for us today to understand what life was like before Social Security. Before 1935, if you were not able to save a fair amount of money during your working life, you simply could not retire. Laborers and farmers, the majority of Americans, were rarely able to save much, if anything. Most of their earning went immediately out for rent, food, clothing, or medicine. And if they did manage to save a little something, they were sure to run into a time of troubles when they had to spend it—the factory closing, a bad harvest, illness.

The result was that most people went on working as long as they could, in the main doing hard physical labor. When they got too old to work they had to depend on relatives, frequently their children, to feed and clothe them. That meant that most people grew up in homes with an aging grandparent, uncle, or aunt living with them. Churches and charities often helped, and many localities had poorhouses and poor farms that took in took in those who had nobody to look after them. But in general the elderly depended upon relatives.

Nor was there any unemployment insurance. If you were out of work you were out of money. We have trouble today grasping the idea that people could actually have no money—not so much as a quarter—and no way of getting any. That was certainly the case at times for millions of Americans during the Depression. That was why people went hungry: They did not have even a dime to buy a little rice or potatoes with.

The idea of Social Security was not invented by New Dealers. The European industrial nations had had such programs for fifty years. Progressives had proposed old-age pensions in 1912, and an unemployment scheme had actually been set up in Wisconsin. Particularly after the Depression began, various people came forward with Social Security plans for the unemployed, the aged, the ill, dependent children, or some combination of these.

President Roosevelt had favored Social Security right along, and in his 1932 election campaign had spoken in favor of it. As the Depression continued, the idea of some kind of unemployment insurance was more and more talked about. By the spring of 1934, several congressmen had introduced Social Security bills. Roosevelt then appointed a committee to study the matter, and the committee debated several different plans. Some people favored state control of unemployment insurance, with the federal government putting up the bulk of the money. Others wanted federal control. Some wanted the money to come from ordinary taxes; others wanted employers, and even employees, to contribute.

Roosevelt, characteristically taking the middle stance, wanted unemployment run by a state-federal partnership. He also wanted the whole system, including old-age benefits, to be paid for out of a fund to which employers and workers would each pay half. There were good arguments against both ideas. For one, if the states were involved, they might all set up different benefit schemes. The idea of having workers contribute, many argued, would establish *regressive* taxation. Ordinary income taxes are usually *progressive*—that is, the more money you make the higher *percentage* you pay. In Roosevelt's Social Security plan, all people would pay the same rate.

But Roosevelt was firm. He said that workers ought to contribute so that they would have "a legal, moral, and political right to collect their pensions and their unemployment benefits." No subsequent Congress, Roosevelt felt, would dare to "scrap my social security program," because the money had been put in by the workers themselves. (The employers would cover their contributions by raising prices, which all consumers—including workers—would end up paying anyway. Under the Social Security system, employees pay Social Security tax on the first certain amount of wages—about $61,000 in 2000—so that lower-income people actually pay a higher percentage than the well-to-do.)

Predictably, conservatives who favored laissez-faire fought against Social Security, calling it a socialist scheme. Industrialists insisted that Social Security would wreck the American system by "destroying initiative, discouraging thrift, and stifling individual responsibility." One of them compared it to the "downfall of Rome." A conservative congressman said it was bound to "prevent business recovery, to enslave workers." On the other side, radicals insisted that the programs provided much too little support for the elderly, the poor, the ill.

But the American people were all for it. In the end all but the most die-hard conservatives in Congress voted for it, and within two years the Social Security Board was deducting payments from wages and collecting money from the employers. A few years later the first beneficiaries began getting monthly checks. Rarely has so massive a program got off to so smooth a start. And few programs have ever represented such a major switch in the philosophy of government. Roosevelt had said, "I see no reason why every child, from the day he is born, shouldn't be a member of the social security system—from the cradle to the grave they ought to be in the social insurance system." The United States was now committed to helping many Americans after their working days were over. (The system did not cover agricultural workers, hotel and restaurant workers, and some other groups.)

Another very important new law pushed by the New Deal government was the National Labor Relations Act, usually known as the

Wagner Act after Senator Robert Wagner, who sponsored it. There are a number of elements in the Wagner Act, but at the heart of it lie rules allowing workers to form unions, permitting strikes, and requiring employers to bargain with union leaders over questions of pay, hours, and working conditions. There were a number of side matters in the act, but these were all to make sure that employers could not undercut unions by devious means, or fire workers for trying to organize unions. The Wagner Act remains the cornerstone of American labor law; without it, it is likely that unions would never have gained much power at all. In 1935 another public works program under the Works Progress Administration (WPA) gave jobs to thousands of men to build schools, post offices, and other public buildings. Artists, writers, actors, and other professionals were also put to work plying their crafts for public benefit.

Inevitably, such dramatic changes in the philosophy of government were bound to awaken much resentment and resistance. As noted, the primary foes of the New Deal were businessmen—owners and managers of corporations, bankers, people who insisted that the old laissez-faire policy had worked before and would work again if government would keep its hands off business. Many ordinary people, too, were conservative at heart, and felt it was wrong, indeed immoral, for people to take handouts from the government. Newspapers, magazines, and radio stations (there was no television then) tended to support the business viewpoint, in part because owners of such media were themselves businessmen, in part because the advertising their profits depended on came mainly from businesses; and in part out of philosophical commitment to the traditional American free enterprise system. Also, a good many Americans were "states' righters," and just on that basis did not like to see the federal government taking so many powers away from the states.

Finally, during the 1930s there were rising to power in Europe dictators like Adolf Hitler in Germany, Benito Mussolini in Italy, Franco in Spain, and others elsewhere who were trampling on their citizens' rights.

In the 1930s, just as Roosevelt was pushing through his novel measures, dictators were arising in Europe, among them Mussolini in Italy, Franco in Spain, and Hitler in Germany, shown here. Many Americans feared that Roosevelt wanted to become a dictator, too.

Some people believed that Roosevelt was on the way to becoming just such a dictator, and opposed him on that ground. But the biggest foe the New Deal had, for a time at least, was America's own Supreme Court.

The American Constitution is in many ways a vague document, with a lot of things unsaid. It does not say that the Supreme Court has the power to declare laws unconstitutional. However, almost from the beginning, the Court took on that power—wisely, most people think.

Supreme Court justices are not gods, but men and women with their own feelings and beliefs. For some time before the Depression the justices had actively supported the laissez-faire idea that the government did not have the power to intrude into business affairs. By the time of the New Deal, six of the nine justices were still committed to that position. Foes of the New Deal knew this, and almost from the first, would challenge New Deal measures in the federal courts. The Supreme Court at times accepted New Deal measures, but often declared them unconstitutional.

They offered many reasons for these decisions, but underlying them was their belief that if the Constitution did not clearly give the national government a certain power, only the states could exercise that power—though they often denied the states the right to control business and labor conditions. Of course, it would have been next to impossible to get all of the states to simultaneously put through New Deal measures.

The best known of these cases involved the National Industry Recovery Act, or NIRA. Cases concerning the NIRA were brought before the U.S. Supreme Court. In the end the justices concluded that the NIRA in effect turned the making of law over to these industry combinations, and through them to the president, who had the last word on decisions. The Court declared that this gave to the president legislative powers that belonged to Congress. Congress may have agreed to the NIRA, but the Supreme Court has usually held that Congress can't give away its power. It did so in this case and central—but generally unsuccessful—sections of the NIRA were declared unconstitutional. Other parts, such as section 7a, which became the Wagner Act, were saved, however.

Several other major New Deal programs were also struck down by the Supreme Court. One historian has said, "Never before had the Supreme Court worked such havoc with a legislative program as it did in 1935 and 1936. . . . " Many of these decisions were reversed by later Courts, which suggests that Roosevelt was probably right, and the Court wrong. Roosevelt grumbled, but for the moment kept his peace with the Court.

As the 1936 elections approached, Roosevelt toured the nation giving election speeches, and huge crowds poured out to greet him. His popular appeal was immense. Masses of people saw him as their savior, the man who was not just saving the nation but themselves personally. No president since Washington, not even Lincoln, has enjoyed such deep and long-lasting adulation in his lifetime as Franklin Roosevelt did. Even though the nation was still frozen in the grip of the Depression, Roosevelt had brought to Americans a spirit of hopefulness; things were bad, but he would make them better. By this time even many businessmen had come to support Roosevelt. In 1936 the voters swept Roosevelt into the White House again. They also gave him an overwhelmingly Democratic Congress. Roosevelt believed, probably correctly, that it had been a personal triumph, that the people had voted for him, not merely for his programs or for the Democratic Party. He now felt strong enough to take on the Supreme Court. He decided to ask Congress to let him enlarge the Court from nine to up to fifteen justices. Roosevelt, of course, would pick the new justices.

The Constitution does not say how many justices the Supreme Court must have, and the number has varied, from five to ten, although it has always had nine since 1869. Roosevelt's proposal would authorize him to appoint one new justice for every one who turned seventy years old and did not retire, so long as the Court did not exceed fifteen members. (In 1936 six justices were over seventy.) A great storm broke out over Roosevelt's "court-packing" plan. It seemed as if Roosevelt were trying to tamper with the independence of the judiciary. Even many of his ardent supporters were opposed. Recall that Americans were watching European dictators like Hitler rise to supreme power by manipulating their constitutions. Roosevelt fought hard for it, giving many talks and speeches, but by mid-1937 it was clear that the court-packing plan would not pass Congress. Roosevelt gave up. Yet a great many Americans had been for it. For the remainder of Roosevelt's presidency, the justices were more tolerant of New Deal measures than they had been, especially since Roosevelt soon got to appoint five new justices to replace those who retired.

Yet despite everything, despite a strong, charismatic president and sweeping legislation, the Depression would not go away. The improvements to the economy that had come during Roosevelt's first administration were swept away by a new recession in 1937. By 1940 the country

The Supreme Court in 1937. Many of the justices were elderly, and held conservative opinions they had acquired in an earlier era. Almost by instinct some of these justices disliked Roosevelt's New Deal measures.

was somewhat better off than it had been ten years earlier, but millions were still out of work, those working were underpaid, some children were still going without shoes, proper food, and medical treatment.

The end of the Depression began in 1940. World War II had started in Europe, and Roosevelt was determined to help Britain and France against the dictators Hitler and Mussolini. American factories began to turn out war materials, putting people back to work. Then on December 7, 1941, the Japanese bombed the American naval base at Pearl Harbor in Hawaii. The United States was now in the war. The government began borrowing billions of dollars to buy arms, and the factories began to run at full speed. Suddenly the Depression was over; and although America has had some recessions since, it has never again seen the hard times of

On December 7, 1941, the Japanese bombed the American naval base at Pearl Harbor, in Hawaii, destroying much of the American Pacific fleet. Here flames and smoke pour from the battleships West Virginia *(foreground) and* Tennessee *(in back). From that moment the United States joined in the war; wartime employment ended the Depression.*

the Great Depression of the 1930s. Most economic historians would agree that we have been spared another economic disaster like that because of the measures passed under the New Deal—unemployment insurance, banking regulations, Social Security, aid for farmers, and much more.

Why did the Depression go on for so long? For one thing, as we have seen, certain industries like coal and textiles and agriculture had long-term fundamental problems that couldn't be fixed by passing a law. For a second, despite New Deal programs, the nation's wealth was still unequally distributed—ordinary workers and farmers, who made up the majority of consumers, were hardly getting a fair share of the nation's income, and could not drive the economy up by buying a lot of goods. This, too, was a problem that could not easily be solved by a new law.

Most economists and historians today agree that the country needed a huge amount of deficit spending by the national government. Roosevelt, we remind ourselves, was no radical. He would go along with deficit spending and government intervention only up to a point. Thus, the Depression only ended when the war forced the government into massive deficit spending.

President Franklin D. Roosevelt broke precedent to become the first president to run for a third term—which he won. In 1944 he ran again for a fourth term. (Soon after the war a constitutional amendment was passed preventing presidents from running for third terms.) However, he was sick and aging, and he died in office in April 1945.

Roosevelt is today remembered as a great war leader. But in truth, the changes to government that came under his administration reshaped America. No longer will the American people permit the government to sit idly by while whole sectors of the population go hungry and homeless without raising the issue.

To be sure, many Americans call for an end to big government: In the 1990s presidents announced that the day of "big government" was over. Even so, American government today is far "bigger" than even Roosevelt could have foreseen. Americans may be suspicious of big government, but they would not give up many of the things that it brings, like Social Security, Medicare, unemployment insurance, government testing of new

Campaign buttons from various of Roosevelt's elections. At the time it was legal for a president to run for more than two terms, but no other president had done it, following the tradition of George Washington, who stepped down after two terms, although he could easily have been elected again. Many Americans opposed Roosevelt's third term on principle, but such was his popularity that he won anyway.

medicines, health and safety rules at work, protections to the environment to make sure Americans have clean air and water, and much, much more.

Many of these ideas came out of the progressive period of 1901–17, and had been passed by Congress during that time. A lot of similar programs, like Medicare and aid to the handicapped, were passed long after the New Deal. But the ones passed during the New Deal are basic to the

Roosevelt points to a map during a briefing for reporters during World War II. Roosevelt is remembered as a great war leader, but it was his New Deal that has had a profound and lasting effect on American government.

American system. During the 1930s the country got the "safety net" (as it is called today) we take for granted, by which people in trouble can look to the government for help. Thus Franklin Roosevelt, in America's greatest economic crisis of all time, saved both democracy and capitalism by reforming the free enterprise system.

Major Legislation of the Hundred Days
March 9 through June 16, 1933

Emergency Banking Relief Act (March 9)
Congress confirmed Roosevelt's "bank holiday"; gave president wide authority over currency and gold and silver; expanded authority of Federal Reserve Board; began abandonment of gold standard.

Civilian Conservation Corps Reforestation Act (March 31)
Established CCC providing environmental protection jobs for 250,000 men ages eighteen to twenty-five.

Federal Emergency Relief Act (May 12)
Created the FER Administration, which was authorized to give up to a total of $500 million to states for relief projects.

Agricultural Adjustment Act (May 12)
Attempted to raise prices farmers received for their produce by: 1) setting a standard "fair" price called parity; 2) reducing supply by paying farmers to limit their production; 3) paying for this by taxing the processors of farm produce; 4) also provided funds to help farmers refinance their mortgages. Provisions 2 and 3 were declared unconstitutional by the Supreme Court in *U.S. v. Butler* in 1936.

Thomas Amendment (to the AAA) (May 12)
Authorized the president to reduce the value of currency (which was supposed to have the effect of raising prices) by lowering the

amount of gold backing each paper dollar; to buy and coin as much silver as he thought desirable; and to issue up to $3 billion of paper money (which he did not do).

Tennessee Valley Authority (May 18)
Provided for federal government development throughout the Tennessee River Basin to control floods and soil erosion by building dams that would also produce cheap electric power in order to encourage factories to locate in this impoverished area.

Federal Securities Act (May 27)
Required private corporations that issued stock to register with the Federal Trade Commission (later, the Securities and Exchange Commission) and make public certain financial information.

Gold Repeal Joint Resolution (June 5)
Congress takes the United States off the gold standard by cancelling the gold clause in all federal and private contracts—making contracts payable in anything the U.S. government declared to be legal tender, usually paper money.

National Employment System Act (June 6)
Established a nationwide employment system coordinated with state systems where they existed.

Home Owners Refinancing Act (June 13)
Created the Home Owners Loan Corporation to help nonfarm home owners make their mortgage payments. Terminated in 1936, by which time it had aided a million home owners.

Glass-Steagall Banking Act (June 16)
Expanded the kinds of banks that could belong to the Federal Reserve System, forbade savings banks from dealing in stocks, created the Federal Deposit Insurance Corporation, and allowed banks to open branches.

National Industrial Recovery Act (June 16)
Gave government sanction and enforcement to the "fair competition" codes that industries had been designing since World War I. Intended to keep employment up. Established the National Labor Board to see that workers were allowed to organize unions and bargain collectively. Established the Public Works Administration to fund the construction of roads and public buildings. The industrial code provisions were declared unconstitutional in *Schechter Poultry Corp. v. U.S.* in 1935. The wages and hours and union protections were reinstituted in 1935 under the National Labor Relations (Wagner) Act.

End of the Hundred Days, June 16, 1933.

BIBLIOGRAPHY

For Teachers

Bernstein, Michael. *The Great Depression: Delayed Recovery and Economic Change in America, 1929-1939*. New York: Cambridge University Press, 1987.

Brinkley, Alan. *Liberalism and Its Discontents*. Cambridge: Harvard University Press, 1998.

————. *Voices of Protest: Huey Long, Father Coughlin, and the New Deal*. New York: Alfred Knopf, 1982.

Cooper, John Milton, Jr. *Pivotal Decades: The United States, 1900–1920*. New York: W.W. Norton, 1990.

Cushman, Barry. *Rethinking the New Deal Court: The Structure of a Constitutional Revolution*. New York: Oxford University Press, 1998.

Fausold, Martin. *The Presidency of Herbert Hoover*. Lawrence: University Press of Kansas, 1985.

Flink, James J. *The Automobile Age*. Cambridge: MIT Press, 1998.

Galbraith, John K. *The Great Crash*. Boston: Houghton Mifflin, 1954.

Ginger, Ray. *Six Days or Forever? Tennessee vs. John Thomas Scopes*. Chicago: Quadrangle Books, 1958.

Gregory, James N. *American Exodus: The Dust Bowl Migration and the Okie Culture in California*. New York: Oxford University Press, 1989.

Hofstader, Richard. *The Age of Reform: From Bryan to FDR*. New York: Alfred Knopf, 1955.

Leuchtenburg, William E. *Franklin D. Roosevelt and the New Deal*. New York: Harper and Row, 1963.

Schlesinger, Arthur M., Jr. *The Crisis of the Old Order*. Boston: Houghton Mifflin, 1957.

Sitkoff, Harvard, ed. *Fifty Years Later: The New Deal Evaluated*. New York: Alfred Knopf, 1985.

For Students

Allen, Frederick Lewis. *Only Yesterday*. New York: Harper and Brothers, 1931.

———. *Since Yesterday. The 1930s in America*. New York: Harper and Brothers, 1940.

Blake, Arthur. *The Scopes Trial: Defending the Right to Teach*. Brookfield, CT: Millbrook Press, 1994.

Burg, David F. *The Great Depression: An Eyewitness History*. New York: Facts on File, 1996.

Deutsch, Sarah Jane. *From Ballots to Breadlines: American Women, 1920–1940*. New York: Oxford University Press, 1994.

Freedman, Russell. *Eleanor Roosevelt: A Life of Discovery*. New York: Clarion Books, 1993.

———. *Franklin Delano Roosevelt*. New York: Clarion Books, 1990.

Frost-Knappmann, Elizabeth. *Woman's Suffrage in America: An Eyewitness History*. New York: Facts on File, 1992.

Katz, William Loren. *The New Freedom to the New Deal, 1913–1929*. Chatham, NJ: Raintree Steck-Vaughn, 1993.

Larsen, Rebecca. *Franklin D. Roosevelt: Man of Destiny*. New York; Franklin Watts, 1991.

Leavall, J. Perry. *Woodrow Wilson*. New York: Chelsea House, 1987.

Meltzer, Milton. *Brother Can You Spare a Dime? The Great Depression, 1929–1933*. New York: Facts on File, 1991.

———. *Theodore Roosevelt and His America*. New York: Franklin Watts, 1994.

Millichap, Nancy M. *The Stock Market Crash of 1929*. New York: New Discovery Books, 1994.

Morris, Jeffrey Brandon. *The FDR Way*. Minneapolis: Lerner Pub., 1996.

Schraff, Anne E. *The Great Depression and the New Deal: America's Economic Collapse and Recovery.* New York: Franklin Watts, 1990.

Spangenburg, Ray, and Diane K. Moser. *Eleanor Roosevelt: A Passion to Improve.* New York: Facts on File, 1997.

Trotter, Joe William. *From Raw Deal to New Deal? African Americans, 1929–1945.* New York: Oxford University Press, 1995.

Watkins, Tom H. *The Great Depression: America in the 1930s.* Boston: Little Brown, 1993.

INDEX

Page numbers for illustrations are in **boldface**

JAMES LINCOLN COLLIER is the author of a number of books both for adults and for young people, including the social history *The Rise of Selfishness in America*. He is also noted for his biographies and historical studies in the field of jazz. Together with his brother, Christopher Collier, he has written a series of award-winning historical novels for children widely used in schools, including the Newbery Honor classic, *My Brother Sam Is Dead*. A graduate of Hamilton College, he lives with his wife in New York City.

CHRISTOPHER COLLIER grew up in Fairfield County, Connecticut and attended public schools there. He graduated from Clark University in Worcester, Massachusetts and earned M.A. and Ph.D. degrees at Columbia University in New York City. After service in the Army and teaching in secondary schools for several years, Mr. Collier began teaching college in 1961. He is now Professor of History at the University of Connecticut and Connecticut State Historian. Mr. Collier has published many scholarly and popular books and articles about Connecticut and American history. With his brother, James, he is the author of nine historical novels for young adults, the best known of which is *My Brother Sam Is Dead*. He lives with his wife Bonnie, a librarian, in Orange, Connecticut.